Mr. Rhinehorn

Buck the Mail Carrier

Ballpark Franky

Wilbur Bright   Orzo Bright

Mrs. Longnecker   Monkey Mantle   Lucy Livingood

To College Park, the love of my life

Henry Holt and Company, *Publishers since 1866*
Henry Holt® is a registered trademark of Macmillan Publishing Group, LLC
120 Broadway, New York, New York 10271 • mackids.com

Library of Congress Cataloging-in-Publication Data
Names: Long, Ethan, author, illustrator.
Title: Hello, world! / Ethan Long.
Description: First edition. | New York : Christy Ottaviano Books,
Henry Holt and Company, 2020. | Series: Happy County ; book 1 |
Summary: Introduces the sights and residents of Happy County, where a lot
of things are happening and every day can end on a happy note.
Identifiers: LCCN 2019018649 | ISBN 9781250191755 (hardcover : alk. paper)
Subjects: | CYAC: Community life—Fiction. | Animals—Fiction.
Classification: LCC PZ7.L8453 Hel 2020 | DDC [E]—dc23
LC record available at https://lccn.loc.gov/2019018649

Our books may be purchased in bulk for promotional, educational, or business use.
Please contact your local bookseller or the Macmillan Corporate and Premium Sales Department at
(800) 221-7945 ext. 5442 or by email at MacmillanSpecialMarkets@macmillan.com.

First edition, 2020 / Design by Ethan Long and Vera Soki
Artwork created with graphite pencil on Strathmore drawing paper, then scanned and colorized digitally.
Printed in China by Toppan Leefung Printing Ltd., Dongguan City, Guangdong Province

1 3 5 7 9 10 8 6 4 2

HELLO, WORLD!

words and pictures by Ethan Long

Christy Ottaviano Books

HENRY HOLT AND COMPANY

New York

Contents

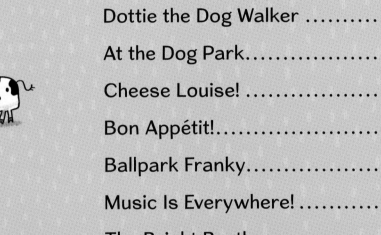

It's a lovely morning in Happy County!
Everyone is up and doing their thing.

Buck the Mail Carrier has started his deliveries,
Mr. Grizzles and Ms. Green are bird-watching, and the
Bright Brothers are testing out their new flying contraption.
Fantastic!

Greetings!

This is Tina Tusker, our County Commissioner. She is in charge of making our county run smoothly.

You can call me the Commish!

Working alongside the Commish is Marcy the County Treasurer. She keeps track of the county's money.

This is Judge Hippstein. He is a tough judge but treats everyone fairly. He loves to use his gavel.

TAP TAP TAP TAP TAP TAP TAP TAP TAP TAP TAP TAP TAP

Debbie Katner publishes the county website. It's called *The Happy Times*.

Miss Beverly is the Head Librarian. She makes sure all the books are in tip-top shape.

Happy County has its own safety patrol, too. They're called the County Mounties!

♪ County Mounties, we're the best!
We wear badges on our chest!
Serve and protect is what we do!
Time to catch that kangaroo!

Thanks, County Mounties! You sure are good singers!

This is Lucy Livingood, our super-duper volunteer. She always makes time to lend a helping hand, wherever it is needed. And of course, she always has a positive attitude.

Looks like the water tower needs a little rakin'!

The Scenic Route

This is Happy County's beautiful countryside.
Look! There's a deer! And a beautiful, sparkling lake!
What else do you see?

Bird Search

Can you help Mr. Grizzles and Ms. Green
find the birds they are searching for?

ROBIN

WREN

BLUE JAY

CHICKADEE

CARDINAL

WOODPECKER

GOLDFINCH

CUCKOO

Do you see anyone else hiding in the bushes?

HUMMINGBIRD

SPARROW

NUTHATCH

WARBLER

SCARLET TANAGER

SWALLOW

BUNTING

ORIOLE

15

She has a hoagie . . .

a hockey puck . . .

and a hula skirt.

Where is Hannah's hammer?

Hannah scratches her head.

Hmm.

Um, Hannah?

Ha! Silly Hannah.

TAP TAP TAP

Hooray! A hook for my one hundred hats!

Hmm. One hook won't hold all those hats.

That's why they have hardware stores, Hannah. You'd better head out for more hooks!

Our Town

Many folks in Happy County choose to live in neighborhoods where lots of other folks are doing lots of different things.

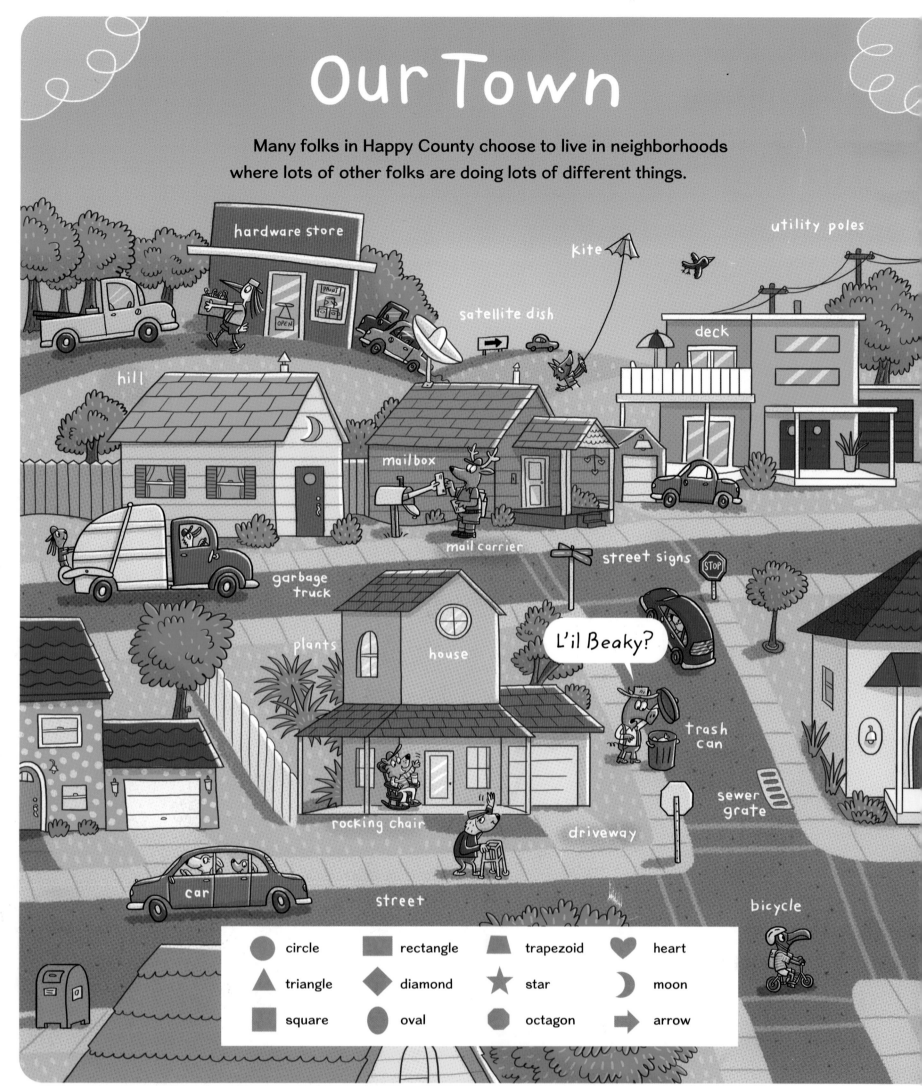

Look! It's Buck the Mail Carrier. And there's Dottie, who loves walking dogs! Do you see Mr. Rhinehorn unpacking his new hammock?

bushes

roof

kangaroo

dog

crosswalk

cul-de-sac

tree

ladder

shed

grill fence

lawn mower

garage

swimming pool

Cheep! Cheep!

fire hydrant

Our town is filled with many shapes, colors, and patterns. Do you see some?

red	green	gray	pink
yellow	blue	magenta	stripes
orange	violet	teal	polka dots

It's Nap Time!

Mr. Rhinehorn's hammock is a nice one.
It is perfect for an afternoon nap.

Hanging it between two trees is a great idea.

But not today.
CHICKA CHICKA CHICKA CHICKA CHICKA

I need the car, dear.

Poor Mr. Rhinehorn! Will he ever find a quiet, dry, uninterrupted spot to take his nap?

Of course he will!

Neighborhood Noises

Good thinking, Mr. Rhinehorn! There's nothing like sleeping in your own bed!

Here are some other neighborhood distractions that Mr. Rhinehorn is thankfully avoiding.

There is always new construction going on in Happy County—cranes, dump trucks, and cement mixers all working to make things bigger and better. Making things better is called "progress" . . . and progress can be very noisy!

At School

Our schools are the best.
Our teachers are top-notch.
The students study hard and
pay attention . . . for the most part.

They also make art . . .

and check out library books, just like you!

Hi, Miss Beverly!

What are they working on today?
It looks like Mrs. Longnecker's class is
practicing their spelling words!

Can you spell these words from memory?	These words are a little bit harder.	If you can spell these, you are a spelling whiz!
me	wave	cheese
do	bird	rough
mom	love	people
dad	tree	pencil
go	nose	giraffe
you	foot	sharp

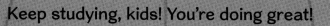

Keep studying, kids! You're doing great!

Dottie the Dog Walker

Dottie just opened a dog-walking service. She starts with one dog.

1

Mrs. Bearbear calls. Now Dottie walks two dogs.

2

Three dogs are good for business. Thank you, Dr. Moosey.

3

Four dogs make things interesting, that's for sure.

4

Five dogs are a handful, to say the least.

5

But six dogs?

6

Seven dogs?

7

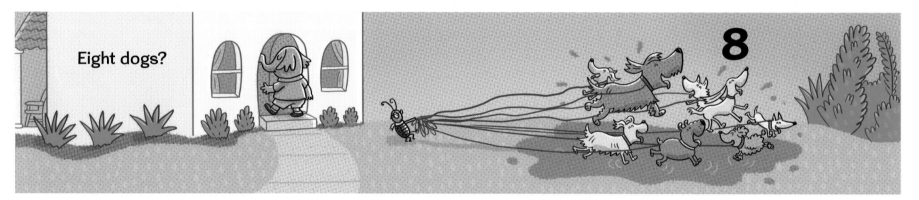

Eight dogs?

8

Nine dogs?

9

CHEEP! CHEEP.

Ten dogs?!
That's too many dogs, Dottie!

HELLLLLLP!

10

Hooray, Dottie! You found yourself a helper!
Now dog walking is fun again!

At the Dog Park

fetch

shed

Taking a dog to the dog park is always a good time. There are many different breeds. A breed is a type of dog. Dogs can do all sorts of things!

greet

ride

stand

roll over

run

dig

stay

Cheese Louise!

Meet Louise, who loves cheese.

But Louise is never at ease.

Do not sneeze near the cheese!

The cheese is not here to squeeze!

Do not leave your keys on the cheese!

Customers are hard to please when you seize all the cheese . . .

NOT FOR SALE

CLOSED

which can lead to a cheese-selling freeze.

CHING!

Buy some cheese!

Pleeeeeease?!

Bon Appétit!
(Some places to EAT!)

Happy County has all kinds of places to eat. What is your favorite food? Can you match the restaurant name with the corresponding sign?

RE-ELECT
TINA
TUSKER
HAPPY COUNTY
COMMISSIONER

Cheep?

ALL
U
CAN
EAT!

MADE
FRESH

OPEN

- Doughnut Den
- Mooshy Sushi
- Sweaty's Spaghetti
- Sally's Salads
- Chicken Legs "R" Us
- Cheese Louise
- Burger Bungalow
- Hal's Hot Dogs
- Pizza Pie Palace
- Steak 'n' Cake
- Taco Timmy's
- Jumbo's Shrimp
- Candy Corn Castle
- Fish Stick Funhouse
- Pee Wee's Popsicles
- Broccoli Barn

MARY'S DAIRY

This guy needs a better business plan.

YUCK!

MUSIC FESTIVAL

Ballpark Franky

Music Is Everywhere!

There is nothing like a music festival to bring joy to the folks of Happy County! Sing along with the musicians as they perform this very familiar song. Come on, you know how it goes!

A-B-C-D

E-F-G

H-I-J-K

L-M-N-O-P

Music brings everyone together.
Look! Even L'il Beaky is back
where she belongs!
Nice work, Farmer Del!

The Bright Brothers

The Bright Brothers have patents for many things. A patent is a license to make, use, or sell an invention.

Their latest invention is a cross between a blimp and a helicopter. It's called a Blopter. At the moment, they are taking the Blopter for a test flight. Up, up, up they go!

Actually, they are not real brothers.
They are buddy brothers. And they are
baseball fans.

LOOK OUT!

PSSSSSSSS!

An exciting game is underway at Crankee Stadium. The home team is eager to score some runs.

But there is a big hole in the Blopter. The Bright Brothers are stuck on home plate!

Monkey Mantle, the star player, stares them down. "Mooooooove!" says the cow catcher.

41

In Happy County, you can end every day on a happy note. So long!

"Then Jesus said to them, 'Watch out! Be on your guard against all kinds of greed; life does not consist in an abundance of possessions.'"

And he told them this parable: "The ground of a certain rich man yielded an abundant harvest. He thought to himself, 'What shall I do? I have no place to store my crops.' Then he said, 'This is what I'll do. I will tear down my barns and build bigger ones, and there I will store my surplus grain. And I'll say to myself, 'You have plenty of grain laid up for many years. Take life easy; eat, drink and be merry'. But God said to him, 'You fool! This very night your life will be demanded from you. Then who will get what you have prepared for yourself? This is how it will be with whoever stores up things for themselves, but is not rich toward God.'"

Luke 12: 15–21 (NIV)

The Princesses' Journal

This story reminds us of another story—one our father has read to us many times. It is found in Luke 12:15–21 and is the parable of the Rich Young Ruler. Our daddy taught us that giving and sharing is necessary to being a true princess. We forgot that lesson when we saw all the decorations and presents. When Father left in full battle regalia and we were in danger, it caused us to stop and think. The robbers entering the castle, and the village being left in shambles, made us realize our greedy hearts needed a change! We needed to walk our talk. We had been concentrating on the immediate and what Christmas would bring US! God focuses on the eternal. He led the way and set the example for us. He gave the greatest gift ever given! He gave EVERYTHING He had … His only Son, as a baby … to grow up and then give His life in our place! Christmas is a time of giving and reflecting Jesus to others. How will you bring Him glory on Christmas?

"Daddy, sing Mother's favorite Christmas carol for us!" And so the king, in his rich baritone began the first stanza of "Joy to the World" while snow fell gently on the kingdom. It truly was a Christmas they wouldn't forget!

Later that night at the palace, the king gathered his five princesses around their not-so-decorated Christmas tree to open presents. He handed each girl one special gift. Surprisingly, no one noticed that there was just *one* gift each.

"So girls, it's tradition time. Let's open your Mother's Bible and read the Christmas story," Father said, as he reached for the beautiful Bible sitting in its place of honor on the mantle.

"Father," called Princess Hope, "we will *not* be needing a larger storehouse for our decorations after all. Christmas means giving to others, not storing up for ourselves."

The princesses surprised the village that Christmas day by decorating their houses and passing out gifts. The townsfolk were honored by their sweet generosity. Passing by the church, the princesses were amazed to find the nativity scene had not been harmed in the slightest and continued to tell the Christmas story of long ago.

"I cannot thank you enough for protecting the princesses and staff. Perhaps the best reward would be early knighthood," the king exclaimed.

The young squires jumped for joy. To be officially knighted by the king would certainly be their best Christmas gift ever!

As many of the castle decorations were loaded onto wagons with food and gifts galore, the king thanked Timothy, Alexander, Christian, Jonathan, and Andrew for their incredible courage. "God bless you, boys! You are brave beyond your years!"

"Thank you, your Majesty," Sir Andrew respectfully responded.

"We are honored to serve you," Sir Alexander said, bowing.

At dawn, the king and his troops, who had fought bravely, finally returned home, victorious! The princesses were so grateful to see their father. But the girls were troubled by news that the village was in turmoil. Bandits had stolen many precious items and parts of the village had been burned.

"What kind of Christmas will the villagers have now?" Princess Faith asked.

"Many of their gifts were taken and decorations destroyed," the king explained.

"We have so much here in the castle, Father. Could we take our Christmas to the village?" Princess Hope requested thoughtfully. And all the girls joyfully agreed.

"You are true princesses, my daughters! What is Christmas without sharing and giving?" The king smiled, proud of his girls.

"We had been tracking these men from the village when they broke away from the others. They probably saw the king leave and thought the castle would be unprotected," Timothy explained.

"We knew they were up to no good, your Highnesses," Christian blustered, as he finished untying the princesses' ropes.

"I was just about to wiggle out of my ropes. I would have gotten them then!" Joy announced waving an invisible sword. Everyone laughed, happy that no harm had come to anyone.

"Wait until we tell father!" Princess Grace said.

Before any real harm came to the girls, the five young squires, with palace guards right behind them, bolted into the room. The battle was quick. The young heroes clobbered the menacing men, capturing them in one fell swoop!

Overjoyed, the princesses and servants thanked the brave squires.

Whispering, Princess Hope said to her sisters, "Try to wiggle your hands so we can get loose." Princess Charity did her best, but began to quietly cry, realizing the danger they were in.

The door suddenly crashed open. The princesses screamed in fear. Their trivial thoughts of presents and Christmas decorations ceased to matter. They trembled as three robbers raced into the kitchen. Hastily, tying up the frightened princesses and castle staff, the dangerous men filled their bags with goods and treasures.

Oblivious to the danger, Joy asked, "Do you think we'll still get to open presents in the morning?"

There was a silent pause. "I just want Daddy to come home safely," Princess Grace said wistfully. And all the girls nodded in agreement.

"Boom! Boom! Boom!" There was loud banging at the kitchen door.

A hush fell over the castle. The girls huddled in the kitchen with clasped hands and bowed their heads praying, "God, we pray for safety and a quick return of our courageous father."

How they wished Mother were near! They missed her terribly.

"I'm scared," Princess Charity whispered, as she hugged her sister.

"Don't worry, Charity," Princess Faith comforted.

"This will be a Christmas we won't forget!" Hope whispered.

"Bang … Snap … Clack … Crash!"

The princesses awoke to a loud clatter. They heard their father giving orders from the foyer below. Leaping up, the girls ran down the steps, halting at the bottom of the staircase.

"Father, what's happening?" Princess Hope called.

"Daughters, do not be frightened. We are on alert. There is an evil band of marauders in the village coming toward the castle. Blow out all the lamps and stay together in the kitchen. I will leave guards outside to protect you."

The girls watched the king abruptly mount his horse and slip into the night. Then they ran to obey their father's wishes.

That night the princesses fell asleep whispering and giggling as they cuddled together for a slumber party in Grace and Faith's room. Outside their window, high in the sky, a lone star shone bigger and brighter than all the others, lighting up the whole countryside that Christmas Eve.

Still buzzing about Christmas morning, the princesses joined their father for a scrumptious yuletide dinner. Princess Hope was explaining to father the need for a larger storehouse for all the decorations.

The king frowned as he listened. He tapped his glass with a fork, calling for their attention to stop and pray. "Father God, thank you for your many blessings … this food, our home, your love. Let us not forget your Son, Jesus, who came to us so long ago. Help us to remember His birth and sacrifice … Amen."

The princesses quickly resumed their frivolous chatter about what they wanted, needed, and hoped was under the Christmas tree.

As she led the group into the grand castle everyone could see the touches of glitter and sparkle everywhere.

"Isn't our tree magnificent?" Grace asked.

"Yes . . . is by far the biggest, most impressive tree I've ever seen," Jonathan proclaimed.

"I cannot wait until tomorrow morning when we open all our presents!" Charity squealed, as she clapped her hands.

After their treat, the squires saddled their horses and rode out of sight shouting, "Merry Christmas to all! And to all a good night!"

"Next year, boys, we have to build a larger storehouse for all the decorations," announced Princess Hope to the kingdom's fearless squires who were helping with the decorating.

"We have so many new ornaments and trimmings they no longer fit," Princess Faith said.

"How many days did it take to put this up?" Sir Alexander wondered out loud.

When the decorating was done, Hope smiled. "Thank you for your help today, kind sirs. Won't you join us inside for hot chocolate?"

A blanket of powdery snow covered the castle walls. The princess sisters found themselves in a scene right out of a fairytale. The most spectacular winter wonderland in years was showing off its splendor. The already picture perfect castle was decorated beyond belief with Christmas finery. With only one day left to wait, the princesses anticipated the best Christmas yet!

Once upon a time, in a magnificent castle perched high on a hill above the sea, there lived five princesses. Their names were Joy, Grace, Faith, Charity, and Hope. They were blessed to be the daughters of the King.

The
Princess
Parables™

A Royal Christmas
to Remember

WRITTEN BY **Jeanna Young & Jacqueline Johnson**
ILLUSTRATED BY **Omar Aranda**

This book is dedicated to the parents who strive to rescue their children from the materialistic focus of this time of year. To those who desire to introduce their child to the person who is "the reason for this season" … Jesus Christ. With deep gratefulness, we acknowledge His enabling, leading, and direction.

J.Y and J.J

ZONDERKIDZ

A Royal Christmas to Remember

Copyright © 2016 by Jeanna Young and Jacqueline Johnson
Illustrations © 2016 by Omar Aranda

Requests for information should be addressed to:

Zonderkidz, 3900 Sparks Dr. SE, Grand Rapids, Michigan 49546

ISBN 978-0-310-74802-1

Editor: Mary Hassinger
Art direction & design: Michelle Lenger

Printed in China

16 17 18 19 / LPC / 22 21 20 19 18 17 16 15 14 13 12 11 10 9 8 7 6 5 4 3 2 1